Jazz and Pop's Adventure

Written by Tarnelia Matthews

Illustrated by Lucy Rogers

Collins

This is Pop.

She has floppy ears, brown bristly fur and a patch on her nose, but she's different to other dogs!

Pop was trained to be my hearing dog and she listens out for the sounds I don't hear because I'm deaf.

As a puppy, Pop lived with a trainer and went to classes to learn new skills. She learnt how to sit and how to fetch.

She learnt not to wriggle and escape at bath time.

As she grew older, she learnt how to listen very carefully. She watched the bustling world, learning about sounds and how to respond.

Once she was ready, Pop was matched to me, to be my hearing dog.

yay!

First thing in the morning, Pop hears my alarm and pats her paws on my bed. This wakes me up, so that I'm not late for school.

When Dad calls me for breakfast, Pop tells me by placing her little paws on my lap and then leads me to the kitchen.

After school, Pop and I go for a walk in the woods with my ball.

The grass is green and vast, like a football pitch.
We feel carefree there.

Pop loves playing ball. She watches as I get ready to start.

With a kick, I launch the ball through the air and she tries to catch it.

Then I strike the ball again, and it goes really far into the trees.

Pop goes tearing across the woods to catch it.
I go racing after Pop. Dad comes running
after me.

Only, once we get to the trees, we can't see Pop or the ball!

I try not to worry but I start to feel scared.
Is Pop lost?

I can see water glistening ahead. We stop and stare, then walk a little closer …

There, in the pond, is Pop – and the ball!

19

Pop comes bustling up to me. I wrap my arms around her and give her a giant squeeze.

I don't care that she's wet and muddy after her adventure. Finding my Pop is worth it.

Jazz and Pop

🐾 Review: After reading 🐾

Use your assessment from hearing the children read to choose any GPCs, words or tricky words that need additional practice.

Read 1: Decoding

- Turn to page 7 and point to **matched**. Discuss what it means in the context of Jazz and Pop being matched. (e.g. *they will get along; Pop's skills will help Jazz's needs*)
- Can the children identify the sound made by the letter "a" or digraph "al" in these words?

  was (/o/)   **ball** (/or/)   **after** (/ar/ or /a/)

  water (/or/)   **watched** (/o/)   **walk** (/or/)

- Point to words on pages 20 and 21. Each time, ask: Can you blend this word in your head when you read it? Encourage them to read the words aloud fluently.

Read 2: Prosody

- Model reading pages 14 and 15, first at a slow speed, and then again, speeding up the pace for page 15 and adding more expression.
- Discuss how speeding up on page 15 emphasises that all the characters are running fast, and helps build excitement into the story.
- Challenge the children to read the pages, adding pace to the short sentences on page 15.

Read 3: Comprehension

- Discuss pet dogs with the children, drawing out their own experiences. Ask: Why do people like dogs? How do they make them feel?
- Focus on the relationship between Jazz and Pop. Reread page 9 and discuss what is special about Jazz's dog. Ask: Why does Jazz need Pop? How does Pop help him?
  - If necessary, return to page 3, and discuss the meaning of **hearing dog** and how Pop uses his hearing to help Jazz.
- Encourage the children to think of ideas for another story about Pop and Jazz, and how Pop helps Jazz by listening for sounds.
  - Talk about sounds that Jazz can't hear at school or at home.
  - Together pick a sound and its cause, and discuss why it's important that Pop lets Jazz know about it.
  - Ask the children what Pop does to help.
- Turn to pages 22–23 and invite the children to tell you what happens in the story, using the pictures as prompts.